From Dream to Reality

The ABC of obtaining a mortgage

By

Mory Friedman

Aron Berger

Zev Spitzer

~ Version II ~

"From Dream to Reality - version II", is now out on the market more ENHANCED and even BETTER for you!

We incorporated in this book most comments and suggestions made by our readers – people like you who read through our book "From Dream to Reality" and offered valuable feedback.

We want to take "From Dream to Reality" to even greater heights.

WITH YOUR INPUT, WE SHALL PERFECT THIS BOOK!

We'd like to have your comments and suggestions:
book@dreammortgagebook.com

Want to speak to us directly?
845-781-2400

Contents:

>> **Preface**

*H*elping people obtain a mortgage to finance the purchase of a home is more than a business. We've been doing this with a passion for almost 15 years. After dealing with hundreds of clients and their individual situations, we realized that many of them would gain immeasurably from a book such as this.

What prompted us to finally write this book?

Over the last several years, we've followed the ups and downs of the mortgage market and rode the waves, just like everyone else. We saw rates as high as nearly 8 percent, and rates as low as nearly 3 percent. (The 18 percent rates our parents used to see didn't show up yet...) We were doing 125% financing with no income verification, and then tumbled into the current mortgage environment where an applicant must have fully documented financial information to get a mortgage, even if the loan is less than 50% of the value of the home. How's that for variation?

Due to these drastic changes in the mortgage field, whenever we get a new potential client, the person usually falls into one of two categories: The first type is a person who obtained a mortgage in the past and expects to get another mortgage just as he did then. This person will be unprepared for all the changes and will be completely overwhelmed by the new stringent regulations.

The second type is a person who never took out a mortgage before and has the notion, based on newspaper dramatizations and hearsay, that it is impossible to obtain a mortgage in today's financial climate.

This is what this book is all about...

Our goal is to educate you, in whichever of the above categories you may belong, so that you should know what you need to do in order to obtain a mortgage with ease. First and foremost, you would need to be prepared with up-to-date information. By knowing what to expect, you will avoid many of the common snags that impede the process. **This book is a vital tool that can help you navigate the mortgage process with peace of mind.**

We tried to include as much information as possible in a clear and concise manner, using simple terms so as not to overwhelm the reader for whom the mortgage jargon is new. Of course, you will still have questions, because each situation is unique. If you feel that a particular subject should have been covered in more detail, or you find that the wording needs clarification, PLEASE do share your comments with us. This book will only become perfect with YOUR feedback. Drop us a note at book@dreammortgagebook.com with your comments, and have your friends do the same. In future editions, we will incorporate your suggestions.

The writing of this book has been a team effort. As the saying goes, "none of us is as smart as all of us." The collaboration of our entire team, who shared their experience, knowledge and insights, took this book from Dream to Reality.

We wish you the best of luck with your mortgage experience!

The mortgage team

Mory Friedman
Aron Berger
Zev Spitzer

>> **Introduction**

*S*hloimy and Raizy are sitting in their tiny kitchen and sharing a late evening snack. Raizy brings up the subject that has been on their minds for the past few months.

"I keep scanning the 'House for Sale' ads and I even circled a number of them. When do you think I should actually begin looking around? Do you think I should contact a real estate agent?"

"I spoke to my friend Yossi, who's a realtor," Shloimy responds. "He started asking me all kinds of questions about my credit and pre-approval and a bunch of other things. From what I understood, it's best to first contact a mortgage broker."

"But they would probably ask me all kinds of questions about the house I'm looking to buy, and I wouldn't know what to answer them before seeing some of the houses on the market."

Shloimy sighed. "That's it, Raizy. If we're serious about buying a house, we should be prepared for these types of things. We'll have to run around a bit but eventually, we'll figure it out."

"Sure, but I wish I could get some kind of manual that would tell me the basics that we need to know in order to turn the dream of home ownership into a reality."

*

Not only first-time home buyers are often clueless about the mortgage process and in need of guidance. People who purchase their second or third property should be aware that a lot has probably changed since the last time they applied for a mortgage. This handy guidebook has been designed to answer your questions and help you plan ahead with confidence.

>> **Credit**

*T*he first thing that a person applying for a mortgage needs to have is a good credit score and a favorable credit history. Any bank lending you money would want to ensure that you would be making your mortgage payments on time. A person earns a good credit score and history by being punctual with their payment obligations. This shows the bank that this person could be trusted with a loan.

There are three credit bureaus that issue credit scores: Transunion, Equifax and Experian. These companies collect information from creditors and lending institutions, and provide a score according to the information they receive. Credit building takes time. Usually, a favorable credit history over a period of 24 months is required.

The best scores are approximately 740-800, but banks will consider lending you money if your credit score is from 660 and higher. The bank will determine your interest rate and loan amount based on your score; therefore it is extremely beneficial to build a good credit score. This can be achieved by paying bills on time, using credit cards regularly (but not having too many credit cards), avoiding using your cards to the maximum credit limit (pref. below 30% of the credit limit), avoiding too many credit inquiries, and similar measures.

When a bank examines your credit, they request a rating from all three companies and will make their decisions based on the middle score.

Credit Inquiries

Each time your credit is looked into, it will be reported on your credit report and it has a minimal effect on your credit score. If there are too many inquiries into your credit, this may negatively affect your score to a greater degree, and sometimes it may even lead to the denial of your loan. This is because when someone has many inquiries, the bank might conclude that the individual is in constant search of more credit and additional loans, which puts him into debt.

A "soft credit inquiry" is a credit pull which you do by yourself, and not through a company or potential lender. A soft credit inquiry is not reported and does not affect your credit score.

Every person may obtain a free credit report once a year and it will not be reflected as a credit inquiry. In fact, it's a good idea to request an annual report and keep a close eye on your credit score. You may obtain your free credit report at www.annualcreditreport.com.

The Ins and Outs of Credit

Every credit card, mortgage, and car loan or lease (called "trade lines") affects your credit. The length and amount of these trade lines matter a great deal. Banks would like to see how long the trade line has been established and if payments were made regularly and reliably. In order to have a favorable credit score you should have at least 3 cards or trade lines with a 24-month history.

When it comes to credit card accounts, if you are the primary account holder or a joint account holder, you are liable for card payments and these accounts reflect on your score. If you are only an authorized user on the account, the card's balances and payments are reflected on your credit report but the banks usually do not count them up in the amount of trade lines that you own.

Even though it is sometimes beneficial for your credit rating to be linked to an additional credit card account as a joint user, you must realize that everything going on with that account will reflect on your credit report, for better or for worse. Be extra cautious not to share an account if the primary user does not make payments on time.

It is important not to let an account move into disputed status, but if it is necessary to take this step, make every effort to clear up the matter. Sometimes, the bank may require a new credit report that reflects no disputed accounts.

Derogatory Credit or negative information on your credit mainly includes, but is not limited to: late payments, collections, judgments, short sales, loans settled for less than the full balance, and bankruptcy. Derogatory credit badly affects the credit score. However, lenders will reconsider lending to people with some types of derogatory credit after a period of time, depending on the situation.

A late payment is reflected on your credit report when it is received 30 days after the payment was due. All collections, even a medical collection, must be paid in full prior to any new closing. When paying up a derogatory credit liability, it is beneficial to retain proof of payment.

• **Stopped Short due to Short Sale** •

When Mr. Miller applied for a mortgage on his second home, he was confident in his ability to receive a loan. He had purchased his first home some years before when the real estate market in his area was inflated and mortgages were easy to obtain. After the collapse of the real estate bubble, his home lost its value. Eventually, he considered opting for a short sale. However, he was concerned about ruining his credit, which would impede his ability to purchase a second home for a fair price.

The firm that advised him to go forward with the short sale assured him that his credit score will not be affected by this process. Mr. Miller was reassured to hear this and after verifying the matter, he proceeded with the short sale.

Some time later, after putting his finances in order and finding a new job, Mr. Miller decided it was time to buy a new home. After looking around a bit, he came across the perfect find: an updated single-family residence in a quiet neighborhood, at a fraction of the price he paid for his first home. He applied for a mortgage, and was shocked at being denied.

"There is a short sale on your credit history," his mortgage broker clarified.

"But the short sale was not supposed to be reflected on my score!" Mr. Miller cried. He was understandably quite agitated and disappointed. "This isn't fair!"

"Please understand," explained the loan officer. "It is indeed true that your credit score remained unaffected by the short sale. However, the bank doesn't just look at your score. They receive a complete credit history and base their decision on that too. Although you still have a high credit score, your credit history is clearly what caused the denial."

• Joint Problem •

Sarah H. decided to apply for a mortgage in order to purchase her first family home. Although she had a good income and felt confident in her ability to pay a mortgage, she lacked an established credit history. In order to help her obtain her mortgage, her brother Ben made her a joint user of his credit card account, linking her to the account's favorable history and helping her establish credit.

This seemed to give her mortgage application a strong push, but unfortunately, it was also her undoing. Ben made a large purchase using his credit card account, but failed to make the payment on time. The interest on his card went up and he had a hard time catching up with the payments. Before long, the account was deeply in the red.

Sarah was blissfully unaware of all this and continued with her mortgage process. Unfortunately, her application was denied due to the derogatory credit of the shared account. What started out as a good idea and gave her hope to build her credit, ended up doing tremendous damage to her credit score and history.

➤➤ Income & Employment

*W*hen the bank considers your mortgage application, one of their primary objectives is to determine whether you will have the ability to make the mortgage payments on time. Though you may have a favorable credit history and plenty of assets, the bank also wants to make sure that you have a stable income that would cover your mortgage expenses without too much difficulty, and that you are gainfully employed.

The income and employment situation that you present in your application must appear sensible to most people. Even if you are somehow able to meet your financial obligations despite not having a regular income or continuous employment, the bank will probably not take a chance. The bank has certain guidelines, and if you don't meet those guidelines, you are bound to have problems.

The bank is very strict with their employment and income guidelines, because if you will fall behind with your mortgage payments they will end up having to take possession of your property. The bank is not a realty company and they are not interested in holding property. Their goal is to lend money to people who pay back according to the payment schedule, without fail.

Employment History

Generally, one must be employed for at least two years, maintaining the same job or position. You can either be a hired worker who earns a regular wage or a self-employed person with your own company or commission-based work. In either case, you would have to prove employment by showing copies of your filed tax returns, W-2 forms, etc.

If a person has two jobs, even if he receives a regular salary and W-2 for both jobs,he would usually need to prove employment at both jobs for two years, without interruption. If a person switched jobs within the last two years, the bank will be more inclined to accept that if both jobs are within the same line of work.

Considerable Income

While most married people file income tax returns jointly, banks only consider the individual income of the one who is applying for the loan. For wage-earners with a W-2 form, they calculate the gross income based on current wages. For self-employed individuals, they calculate the net income – the amount after deductions, as reported on the personal income tax return. This is an important difference to remember. The bank considers a person self-employed if he files a schedule C, has more than 25% ownership in an S corporation, or if he has the position of officer in a C corporation.

Some deductions that are beneficial for a taxpayer may be counted up and considered as income for mortgage qualification purposes.

If a person is employed in a family business or being paid on an hourly basis, the bank will typically consider the income based on an average of the current year-to-date income and the total filed income of the past two years.

Be aware that every increase or decrease in income requires clarification, especially when employed as part of a family business.

The bank may also consider other sources of income such as SSI, foster care, retired income and more government stipends and programs, including Section 8.

A co-borrower or a non-occupant co-borrower on your mortgage may only be an immediate family member.

Each borrower is 100% liable for all mortgage payments and is subject to full underwriting on his credit and income.

• Full Disclosure •

Simon W. applied for a mortgage to purchase a lot that he wished to develop. He was looking forward to go proceed with this promising project and eagerly furnished all required documentation to his loan officer. Upon examining his income, the loan officer saw that Simon was earning nicely, and it was clearly reflected on his W-2 form. It seemed as if he would have no problems in this area.

However, Simon also had partial ownership in a business which was operating at a loss. He felt no need to disclose this side-issue when applying for the loan. Unknown to him, the bank requested a full report from the IRS and discovered his connection to the floundering business. They adjusted Simon's net income to reflect the business' losses and denied his mortgage application.

It is important for applicants to realize that the bank goes directly to the source of all personal income information, and anything less than full disclosure will only hamper the application process.

➤➤ **Assets**

*W*hen purchasing a home, you must invest your own funds to cover the down payment and the closing costs. The down payment is the difference between the loan amount and the purchase price. For example, if you purchase a property for $450,000 and apply for a mortgage for $375,000, your down payment would be $75,000, coming from your own money. The closing costs are all the extra expenses and taxes that come along with purchasing a house and obtaining a mortgage, and can total a significant amount.

The bank will make sure that you have enough funds to pay for the down payment and cover all closing costs. The amount of your down payment will make a difference in determining the interest rate of the mortgage, and will be a strong factor in the application process.

Why does the bank care how much money you invest in the property? This is because, by lending you the bulk of the money for the property, the bank becomes your partner in this venture. They want to make sure that you are committed to the deal and that you have a personal interest in the property. If you do not invest your own money, and everything comes from the bank, then you will not be losing your own money if the mortgage goes into default. On the other hand, if you do invest your own money, you will have a vested interest in paying your mortgage, so as not to lose the savings that you put into the deal. For example, if you invest $75,000 of your hard-earned savings in a down payment, you will not want to lose the property to the bank by not paying your mortgage. Naturally, the bigger the down payment, the more favorable it appears to the bank.

Two more reasons for checking the source of your funds is to make sure that you have no other undisclosed loans, and to ensure that all money used in this transaction is completely legal.

Acceptable Funds

Assets include anything of value that you own. These are categorized in two:

1: General Assets – Real estate properties and buildings in your possession

2: Liquid Assets – Cash values and cash equivalents.

When applying for a residential mortgage, banks will <u>only consider liquid assets and cash funds</u>, but not hard cash from under your mattress or money that you have invested in real estate.

The bank will verify that you have sufficient liquid assets and cash funds that are accessible at the time of closing. Some of the acceptable forms of assets include checking accounts, savings accounts, CD accounts, mutual funds, stocks, bonds, cash value of life insurance, a line of credit against another property, proceeds of the sale of real estate, and brokerage accounts. Gifts from immediate family members are acceptable for primary-residence purchases only. In some cases, you may use business assets.

Some of the non-acceptable asset types include hard cash, non-secured loans, and private loans.

Proof of Funds

Assets must be verified and proven with statements. Since

lenders want to ensure that the assets are your own funds, they will request several consecutive statements.

Each deposit reflected on the statement – except from your payroll or other regular income - needs to be sourced and explained to the bank. This is especially true for large deposits, which will definitely be questioned and an explanation will be required.

• Sudden, Unexplained Deposits Won't Work •

Avi and Reesa Schwartz were working on a mortgage application, and were requested to supply bank statements to show proof of assets. Avi's good friend, a wealthy guy named Mendy, agreed to lend him a significant amount of cash to help him show proof of assets. Mendy transferred $100,000 into Avi's savings account and let it sit there for two months.

When the loan officer requested from the Schwartz's two months of bank statements, they furnished statements that showed a balance of over $100,000. Since the bank generally only looks at the last two months, they were sure that this would be sufficient.

However, the bank officers reviewed the statements more carefully than Avi anticipated. On the bottom of the statements, there was a figure indicating the accumulation of interest. The year to date total interest was much lower than what would normally be paid for such a large account. If the Schwartzes had saved up this money over time in this account, they would have accumulated much more interest in the course of the year.

The bank decided to check into this and researched the account's full history. They quickly realized that the $100,000 balance suddenly appeared via a lump sum payment, the source of which was not readily clear. The money in the savings account was discounted by the bank.

• House Rich •

Yosef purchased a home with a 30-year mortgage. He always dreamed of paying off his mortgage, something he equated with financial freedom. Over the years, whenever he received a bonus at work or saved up a larger amount of cash, he paid it towards his mortgage principle.

After sixteen years, Yosef managed to finish paying off the bank! He was exhilarated at finally being the sole owner of his home.

Several months later, he decided to purchase an apartment for his newlywed children. He was sure the banks would consider him a "good customer." After all, he paid off his first mortgage in nearly half the time of the loan.

There was just one significant problem. Due to having put every penny into his home over the years, Yosef had no savings. When he applied for a new mortgage, he couldn't prove enough assets and the bank denied his application! The money he had invested in his home did not count as acceptable assets in this case.

This is an unfortunate twist of irony in which a person can be house rich but cash poor, and lose out in the end. Sometimes it is indeed a good idea to pay off the mortgage principle to save on interest, but oftentimes a person stands more to lose than gain by doing so, when it comes to future mortgages.

>> Liabilities

Liabilities are financial obligations for which you are liable to pay. Liabilities include everything for which you are accountable – that is, all loans, leases, taxes, etc.

Every single liability is taken into account when applying for a mortgage. This makes sense; even if you earn a respectable income, the bank would like to know if you are in debt from previous mortgages and figure your liability overhead in order to determine if you would be able to meet your new mortgage payments. Therefore, the total of all liabilities is counted against your income. The bank allows for only a limited percentage of the income to cover liability expenses.

The following are some of the liabilities that the bank will consider as debts:

1. Credit card debts, car loans, mortgage loans and student loans. You are obligated to pay the minimum payment every month, and this amount is considered

when tallying up your liabilities. If there is no minimum payment reported, you are in charge of full payment for each month.

2. Child support. When one is liable for child support they need to pay the full monthly obligation.

3. Real estate expenses. This includes all property expenses such as taxes, insurance, condo fees, etc. All property expenses for the subject property – for which you are applying for a loan – are also considered.

Note: all other personal expenses (utilities, health insurance, tuition, etc.) do not have to be reported.

Important to note: all of these expenses are counted as your liabilities, even if you are not the primary account holder who issues the payments. Even if you are only a co-signer on a mortgage, and you do not own the house, the monthly payment is your liability. Likewise, if you are a joint account user on any type of account, you are equally liable for the full minimum payment and the debt is considered to be yours, even if someone else actually makes the payments.

Omitting Liabilities

In some circumstances, liabilities may be excluded and omitted from the total of one's debts. This happens when you bring 12 months of proof that the other joint holder of the account, or your employer, has been paying the obligation. However, if you cannot prove that the other party has been paying it for 12 consecutive months, or if the account has been opened for less than 12 months, this liability cannot be omitted.

When it comes to car loans, there is an important difference between a loan and a lease. A car loan with less than 10 month of payments left does not have to be included among your monthly liabilities. On the other hand, a car lease does have to be included until the lease was surrendered (even if you already paid up the balance).

• Lease vs. Loan •

Mr. Green took out a bank loan for a new car. After an extremely successful sales season in his business, he managed to pay off the loan completely and also paid up the balance of his wife's car lease. When he applied for a mortgage, his car was no longer a liability.

However, his wife's car still counted as a monthly liability for the full monthly lease amount. This is because the bank considers a lease a liability even if further payments no longer have to be made.

>> Value and Price of Property

*T*he bank will determine how much money they are willing to lend you based on their estimation of value of the property. Therefore, the next factor in determining the eligibility of your mortgage application is estimating the true market value of the property being bought, compared to the price of purchase. For example, when applying for a $375,000 mortgage on a property with a purchase price of $450,000, the bank will want to ensure that the price is not inflated, and the property is indeed worth the amount of money being paid. If, according to their assessment, the property isn't worth the full amount, they will not agree to provide you with a mortgage based on a higher price. Once again, this is because the bank wants to ensure that if the mortgage ends up in default and the bank decides to sell the property, they would get back all of their money.

Important! These days, mortgage brokers cannot and do not have any influence over the appraisal of the property. Banks recently banned appraisers from communication about the value in any way.

The appraiser is a certified individual who is qualified to estimate the market value of the property. He gives an expert judgment of the value by comparing the property to recent sales of similar apartments in the area. Generally, his estimation depends more on the average consumer's perception of the worth of the house than on its intrinsic value. A house can have some expensive features that the seller and/or buyer feel are important, but the appraiser would be more inclined to base his estimation on the preferences of most purchasers.

Due to this, it is important to learn the value of the unit before negotiating a contract price. This is because you can only get financing according to the bank's estimation of the property's value. If you settled for a contract of $550,000 but the appraiser estimates that the property is only worth $475,000, the bank will only provide you with a mortgage up to $475,000, less the required down payment.

• Too Quick Contract •

The Blooms went house hunting and after seeing a number of houses, a particular house seemed to be everything they've ever wanted in a home. The house's color was Mrs. Bloom's favorite, and it had a dainty white fence surrounded by rose bushes and flower beds. The house had a lovely study that captured Mr. Bloom's fantasy right away. There were other details in the house that made this the perfect choice for the Bloom family.

The seller's price was $400,000, which the Blooms felt was fair and reasonable, given the many advantages they saw in the house. They signed contract and began the mortgage process.

The appraiser came down to evaluate the house and appraised its value to be $350,000. This is because the appraiser did not count the location of the study or the color of the home's exterior, but based his calculations on the average market value of similar homes in the area. Due to this, the bank refused to provide more than $350,000 in financing, less the down payment.

The Blooms really wanted the house very badly, but in order to buy it they would have to come up with another $50,000, above the amount they had originally saved up for the down payment.

>> **RECAP of the Mortgage Requirements**

H *ow do I qualify for a mortgage?*

There are four main components in the mortgage qualification process.

- **Credit**

- **Income**

- **Assets**

- **Property**

Following is a brief description and summary. These components are explained and demonstrated in length in the chapters of the book.

Credit

How do I prove to the bank that I am reliable to make my mortgage payments on time?

A good credit history and score are essential to be approved for any loan. Insufficient credit which includes a short credit history or bad credit such as late payments, collections and judgments appearing on your credit may result in your loan being denied by the bank.

Read the Credit chapter in the book for a detailed description on credit requirements.

Assets

How will I pay for the down payment and closing cost of my loan?

You need sufficient money to cover the intended transaction. If you need a mortgage to buy your home, you must put in your portion of the deal: The remaining balance of the purchase price, which is the down payment, as well as the closing costs. For refinance transaction, you may also need assets if the new loan combined with closing costs is insufficient to pay off the existing loan. In some cases you will also need some reserves assets in addition to what is needed to cover the transaction.

Any of the following is a good source of assets:

- Checking or saving account statements – It must be in your name; large transactions must be explained and sourced.

- Life insurance cash value, IRA accounts, stocks & mutual fund etc – Funds will need to be liquidated and trailed to the closing if needed for the transaction.

- Gifts – In some cases a gift from a relative can be a source of accepted assets.

Income

How much income do I need, or better yet, what does my current income qualify me for?

In general, 43% of your total monthly income needs to cover all your monthly liabilities, which includes all of the following:

- All mortgage payments, including the new loan.

- All minimum monthly credit card, car lease, student loan payments.

- All real estate tax, Hazard insurance payments, for all real estate owned.

The bank will review the last two years of your tax returns to determine your income as well as the probability that the income will continue. [In some cased though, one year tax returns will be enough]. Large increases in income or drastic changes in employment type, such as being a Rabbi this year and a car mechanic the other year, might result in the loan not being approved. Likewise the bank may feel uncomfortable that this employment will continue and insecure with the income altogether.

Property

On which property do you want to get mortgage financing and how much is it worth?

The property on which you are applying to get a mortgage will certainly be appraised by the bank, and a title company will search for liens and violations against this property. The unit will need to be appraised to get its desired value in order to be approved for the applied loan amount. The appraisal and title company will also determine if the property is used in a legal matter. For example, a 2-family unit being utilized as a 3-family unit is an illegal usage and it will not be acceptable.

>> **The Mortgage Process**

*F*inally, we're ready to discuss the actual mortgage process.

Most of us are used to walking into stores and purchasing whatever we want or need with ease. We use our own judgment to estimate if the item is worth its price, and we make our own decisions if we would like to pay for it or not.

Before purchasing a house, it is important to realize that this process is nothing near regular store-shopping. Applying for a mortgage is an extensive process that involves many steps along the way. Snags inevitably come up and it could be quite stressful. The buyer cannot make his own decisions; ultimately, the bank will decide if the property is worth its price and if they agree to go into partnership with you.

As in every situation, knowledge is power. If you are informed about the process, know what to expect and are prepared to comply with the requirements, you stand a good chance of acquiring a mortgage with relative ease and purchasing the home of your dreams.

1. Pre-approval

Most real estate brokers would want you to pre-qualify for a mortgage before they show you around and spend time "house shopping." This is because often they invest many hours in a potential client, only to find out that the individual does not qualify for a mortgage and cannot buy a house. To avoid this frustration, they expect you to prove pre-eligibility to show that you're a serious buyer.

When a person is being pre-qualified for a mortgage loan, the following three things are being determined: a) If he would be able to obtain a mortgage at all, b) the maximum amount he can borrow, and c) for what amount of money he can afford to purchase the property. After going through with the pre-approval, the buyer should have a good idea in what price-range the house he buys should be, and how large his down payment must be.

Prequalifying includes: credit check, an overview of income, and verification of assets.

Some sellers require the person to be pre-qualified for a mortgage prior to signing contract. It is best to begin this process as soon as you begin to think of purchasing a property, to avoid complications later in the game.

So, to answer the question of most first-time home buyers if they should first look around and see what's on the market or speak to a mortgage broker first - it is best to do the pre-approval as soon as you think of buying a house, even before you contact any realtors.

2. The Application Process

Initial Application

Once you sign an official contract, provided that the apartment will be ready within the next three months, the application is actually initiated. The mortgage broker then gathers all information to complete the application and the borrower supplies the required supporting documentation.

Processing Review

The broker evaluates the entire package of loan information once again to ensure that everything is complete. Then the file is submitted to the bank for Underwriting Review.

Underwriting Review

The underwriters at the bank are responsible for determining whether the combined package passed over by the processor is deemed acceptable for a loan. If more information is needed, the borrower is contacted to supply more documentation or explanation.

Conditional Approval

The bank will approve the loan based on information they received, and on the condition that they will get the additional documents and conditions they request after the file review. Once the borrower provides the additional required documentation, the file goes back to the underwriters for final approval and clearance.

Locking the Rate

Before scheduling the closing, the rate must be locked. The rate lock will then affect and determine the precise, final amount of your monthly mortgage payment. Because you arrive at this step only after the application has been activated, you cannot be sure of the exact monthly mortgage payment you will end up with, until you reach this point. This is because the interest rate fluctuates on a daily basis and ultimately, the rate you get in the end depends on the day you lock it.

Title

An attorney reviews the title report to check if it is clean from violations and liens against the property. Likewise, they ensure the property against any kind of fault.

3. Closing

At the closing, the lender (bank) funds the loan with a check to the seller, in exchange for the title to the property. This is the point at which the borrower finishes the loan process and actually buys the house.

Mazel Tov!

>> **Facts You Should Know**

*H*ome mortgages are usually loaned for a 30 year period, but are also available for 25, 20, 15 & 10 years. Although the bank may charge a lower interest rate for a loan with lesser term, mortgages that run for fewer years are absolutely more difficult to obtain, because the monthly mortgage payments are higher and more income is required in order to qualify.

Most mortgage plans come with a fixed rate that remains unchanged for the full duration of the loan, regardless of how interest rates fluctuate during that time.

The interest rate is the percentage that the borrower will pay on the loan each month. The rate is determined by certain risks to the loan. This means that if the bank considers this a loan with relatively minor risk, they would usually offer a lower interest rate. With every increase in risk to the loan, the bank will increase the interest rate to offset that risk.

Some of the things that affect the interest rate are:

- Your credit score

- Whether you plan to occupy the property and make it your primary residence, or secondary home, or if you purchase it as an investment

- Whether the transaction is a purchase or refinancing

- The length of the rate-lock period

- The percentage of the loan amount compared to the total value of the home

Private Mortgage Insurance

There are private insurance companies that protect lenders against a loss. When a loan amount exceeds 80% of the home value (meaning that your down payment is less than 20% of the purchase price), the bank sees this as a risk. In such cases, the bank will require the borrower to obtain Private Mortgage Insurance (PMI) to protect the lender from incurring a loss. The monthly premium will be included in the mortgage payment. If your down payment is at least 20% of the purchase price, this PMI requirement is removed and is no longer needed.

You can request to remove the PMI when the loan amount reaches 80%; whereas, banks are required to remove this insurance when it is 78% of the value.

Closing Costs

The estimated closing cost is listed in the Good Faith Estimate provided by the bank or loan officer. The total cost of closing includes bank fees, title fees, first month of mortgage interest and escrows. Title fees are charged by a separate title company and are beyond the control of the bank or mortgage broker, although the broker will provide you with the estimated charges.

The only charge that can make a significant difference is the upfront broker fee, which varies greatly between mortgage brokers.

The following is a listing of charges that are included in the closing costs:

1. Bank fees – including an underwriting fee and the bank attorney's closing fee.
2. Title fees – the bulk of the charges include fees for title insurance, searches, mortgage and transfer tax (which are government fees that are collected by the title company), and recording fees.

3. Recording Fees – A fee collected by the title company for recording real estate and mortgage documents. It is necessary to legally document real estate transactions to ensure accurate records for property ownership and legal purposes.

4. Mortgage interest – this includes the interest for your mortgage from the date of closing until the end of the month. For example, if you close on March 15, you will pay at the closing the interest from March 15 until March 31, and your first mortgage payment will be due on May 1. (Your always pay your mortgage for the previous month.)

5. Escrows – Your mortgage is set to collect your property taxes and insurance premiums. These fees are added to your mortgage bills and are paid by the bank when due. At the closing, the bank will collect about half of the annual taxes and insurance premiums.

6. Broker fee – depending on your arrangement with the mortgage broker. There are brokers who may charge an upfront broker fee (called upfront points), while some brokers won't charge you.

7. Seller's closing charges – some sellers will charge a closing fee. When applicable, it should be outlined in the contract.

8. Tax adjustment – the seller will adjust and charge you for the taxes that were already prepaid.

9. Upfront condo maintenance fee – when purchasing a condo unit in a new development, you will usually need to pay between 3-6 months upfront maintenance fees.

>> Useful Definitions

Appraisal	A written justification of the price paid for a property, primarily based on an analysis of comparable sales of similar homes nearby.
Bank Charge	Charge and fees of bank for providing mortgage financing.
Borrower	The individual that is listed on the loan application.
Broker Charge	Charge and fees of broker.
Co-borrower	An additional individual who is both obligated on the loan and is on title to the property.

Contract price	The price written on a legal contract agreement, which the buyer agrees to pay to the seller.
Closing Costs	All closing cost and fees paid by a borrower at the time of closing.
Down Payment	Difference between purchase price on a legal contract and loan amount.
Escrow	Amount inserted to the escrow account, which will be applied as taxes to make up for the missing months from the closing until the due tax bill.
First Month Payment	This payment is for the interest on your loan from the day of your closing until the first day of the next month.
HUD-1 Settlement Statement	A document that provides an itemized listing of the funds that were paid at closing. The HUD1 statement is also known as the "closing statement" or "settlement sheet."
Homeowner's Insurance	An insurance policy that combines personal liability insurance and hazard insurance coverage for a dwelling and its contents.
Loan Amount	Amount of money a borrower receives from bank at closing.

Loan-to-value (LTV)	The percentage relationship between the amount of the loan and the appraised value or sales price (whichever is lower).
Loan Servicing company	The company that collects the monthly mortgage payments for the bank.
Loan Term	Is the amount of months you will repay the loan.
lock-In	An agreement in which the lender guarantees a specified interest rate for a certain amount of time at a certain cost.
Mortgage	A legal document that pledges a property to the lender as security for payment of a debt. Instead of mortgages, some states use First Trust Deeds.
No cash-out refinance	A refinance transaction which is not intended to put cash in the hand of the borrower. Instead, the new balance is calculated to cover the balance due on the current loan and any costs associated with obtaining the new mortgage. Often referred to as a "rate and term refinance."
Note	A legal document that obligates a borrower.

PITI Amount	Four components (Principal - Interest - Taxes - Insurance) of housing cost that is combined in a single monthly payment that is paid by borrower.
Principal/Interest	The original amount of money borrower, which is paid back with interest.
Refinance	To redo your mortgage for any of the following reasons: to obtain a better rate or mortgage term, to obtain cash out of the deal for debt consolidation or home improvement.
Subject Property Address	The property on which the loan is applied
Title	The legal rights of ownership and possession evidenced by a legal document. A legal title empowers its holder to control the property and serves as a link between the titleholder and the property itself.
Title Charge	Charge and fees of title insurance, government and recording fees.
Taxes/Insurance	The monthly payment to cover 1/12th of annual property taxes and insurance premium and is kept in escrow until due for payment.

>> **Mortgage Calculator**

This Mortgage Payment Table will allow you to estimate your monthly principal and interest payments for any fixed interest rate mortgage. You can't reliably use the chart to calculate the monthly payment for an adjustable rate mortgage, except for the initial period; after that, of course, the rate, the term (and the payments) will be different.

Scan down the interest rate column to a given interest rate, such as 8.875%; then follow across to the payment factor for either a 15 or 30 year term. Multiply the factor shown [10.07 for a 15 year; 7.96 for a 30 year] by the number of thousands in your mortgage amount [such as 235, when the loan amount is $235,000], and the result is your monthly principal and interest payment.

In our example, with a loan of $235,000 and interest rate of 8.875% for 30 years, multiply 7.96 X 235 = $1870.60 per month.

This chart covers interest rates from 8.875% to 2.5%, and loan terms of 15 and 30 years.

Interest Rate %	15 Year Term Monthly Payment	30 Year Term Monthly Payment
8.875%	10.07	7.96
8.75%	9.99	7.87
8.625%	9.92	7.78
8.50%	9.85	7.69
8.375%	9.77	7.6
8.25%	9.7	7.51
8.125%	9.63	7.42
8.00%	9.56	7.34
7.875%	9.48	7.25
7.75%	9.41	7.16
7.625%	9.34	7.08
7.50%	9.27	6.99
7.375%	9.2	6.91
7.25%	9.13	6.82
7.125%	9.06	6.74
7.00%	8.99	6.65
6.875%	8.92	6.57
6.75%	8.85	6.49
6.625%	8.78	6.4
6.50%	8.72	6.33
6.375%	8.64	6.24
6.25%	8.58	6.16
6.125%	8.51	6.08
6.00%	8.44	6
5.875%	8.37	5.92
5.75%	8.31	5.84

Interest Rate %	15 Year Term Monthly Payment	30 Year Term Monthly Payment
5.625%	8.24	5.76
5.50%	8.18	5.68
5.375%	8.1	5.59
5.25%	8.03	5.52
5.125%	7.97	5.44
5.00%	7.9	5.36
4.875%	7.84	5.29
4.75%	7.77	5.21
4.625%	7.71	5.14
4.50%	7.64	5.06
4.375%	7.58	4.99
4.25%	7.52	4.91
4.125%	7.45	4.84
4.00%	7.39	4.77
3.875%	7.33	4.7
3.75%	7.27	4.63
3.625%	7.21	4.56
3.50%	7.15	4.49
3.375%	7.09	4.42
3.25%	7.03	4.35
3.125%	6.97	4.28
3.0%	6.91	4.22
2.875%	6.85	4.15
2.75%	6.79	4.08
2.625%	6.73	4.02
2.50%	6.67	3.95